Guinea Pigs

Laura Howell

❖

Designed by Adam Constantine
and Kate Rimmer

❖

Consultant: Peter Gurney

Illustrations by Christyan Fox
Photographs by Jane Burton

CONTENTS

About guinea pigs

Guinea pigs, also known as cavies, are small, furry animals which originally came from South America. They make gentle and friendly pets, as long as you give them lots of love and attention. This book will help you choose your first guinea pig, and tell you how to take care of it.

How big?

Guinea pigs don't grow very large. An average adult guinea pig is around 25cm (10in) long, and weighs about 1.25kg (2½lb). They live for up to seven years.

This guinea pig has short fur, but there are long-haired varieties, too.

A guinea pig's tail is too short to see.

The ears are small, and fold over a little.

A guinea pig twitches its whiskers and nose when it is curious or alert.

The front paws have four toes, but the back paws have only three.

What's in a name?

No one knows for sure how guinea pigs got their odd name. Some people think it's because they used to be sold for one guinea, an old British coin.

In the family

A guinea pig uses its strong teeth to gnaw food and hard objects.

Guinea pigs aren't related to pigs at all – they belong to a family of animals called rodents, with long teeth for gnawing. Mice and rats are rodents.

For a link to a website where you can find
an interactive guide to guinea pigs, go to
www.usborne-quicklinks.com

Seeing

Guinea pigs can't see
details well, but they are
good at spotting movement.
Their eyes are high up on
their heads, so they see
things above them best.

Hearing

A guinea pig's sensitive
ears can hear many
sounds that yours can't.

*Don't make sudden noises
near your guinea pig, as they
might cause it to panic.*

Smelling

A guinea pig's sense of smell is much
better than a person's. It helps it to
identify friends and enemies, or to
tell if it's in an area that belongs
to another animal.

*If you hold out your
hand and let your
guinea pig sniff, it
will soon learn your
scent and recognize
you as its friend.*

sniff...

sniff...

Living together

Wild guinea pigs live
in groups called herds.
Each herd has one
male guinea pig, called
a boar, and many
females, called sows.

*Guinea pigs feel safer
in a group than on
their own.*

Eating machines

Guinea pigs have
healthy appetites.
In the wild, they
spend up to 20
hours every day
munching grass.
Your guinea pig
will also spend a
lot of time eating.

*This guinea pig
is enjoying
some cabbage.*

Choosing a guinea pig

Guinea pig babies are ready to leave their mother when they are about five or six weeks old. This is the best age to buy a guinea pig, as it will be easier to tame.

Here are some things to look for when choosing your new pet.

Its body should feel plump, not bony.

Check that its teeth are clean and not too long.

Don't buy a guinea pig with cuts, lumps or a rash on its skin.

Make sure the fur is glossy, with no bald patches.

Where to buy

You can buy guinea pigs from pet stores, but it's better to buy from breeders. Animal shelters often have guinea pigs that need loving new homes.

The eyes should be bright, not sticky or cloudy.

The nose should be dry. A runny nose could be a sign of illness.

A healthy, happy guinea pig will be friendly and inquisitive.

How many?

Guinea pigs get lonely very easily, so it's best to buy a pair. Male guinea pigs will probably fight, unless they are from the same family, but females will live together happily. Make sure the person you buy from can tell that they are both the same sex, or they will have babies.

A pair of young sisters will get along best.

For a link to a website where you can find all sorts of information about guinea pigs, go to **www.usborne-quicklinks.com**

What breed?

Long-haired guinea pigs have flowing, silky fur that grows down to the floor. They are harder to take care of than short-haired varieties, because they need so much brushing and combing.

Short-haired guinea pigs are most commonly kept as pets, because they are easy to keep clean. They can have many different markings.

This long-haired guinea pig is having the knots and tangles gently combed out of its fur. This needs doing every day.

Abyssinian guinea pigs have short, tufty fur that grows in flower shaped "rosettes", as shown here. These two babies will develop rosettes as their hair grows.

How to choose

It's a good idea to sit down while you hold the guinea pig, in case it struggles and falls.

Watch all the guinea pigs from a little way away. Don't try to touch them yet.

Look for the most lively guinea pig. Ask if you can be shown how to pick it up.

Hold it and gently stroke it for a while. Decide if you think it's friendly.

What will I need?

Before you buy a guinea pig, there are some essential items that you'll need in order to care for it properly. You can buy all of them from a pet store.

Which home?

The type of home you buy for your guinea pig will depend on where you are going to keep it. You'll need a cage for indoors, or a hutch for outside. Find out more about hutches and cages on pages 8–9 and 16–17.

Bedding

Guinea pigs need something to burrow in, such as clean, shredded paper or bedding for small animals. Never use pine or cedar wood shavings, which can harm your pet's skin, or sawdust, which causes breathing problems. If you buy bedding from a store, make sure the label says it's safe for guinea pigs.

This pet-carrying box has its lid partly open, so you can see inside. A little hay makes it more comfy.

Pet stores sell bags of shredded paper, or you can shred some yourself.

Carrying box

You'll need a box to bring your guinea pig, or guinea pigs, home. This can be made of cardboard or plastic, but make sure it's sturdy and has air holes so the animals can breathe. Put a sheet of paper and some hay in the bottom.

Use newspaper or large sheets of plain paper to line the floor of your pet's hutch or cage.

Gnawing block

Your guinea pig needs to gnaw on hard things to keep its teeth from growing too long. Pet stores sell blocks that are safe for animals to chew, but any piece of hard, unpainted wood will do.

Water

If you put water in a bowl, it will quickly become dirty. Instead, use a drip-feed bottle that attaches to the side of the cage. Don't let the spout's end touch the hay and bedding, or it will leak.

Hang the water bottle at a comfortable height for your guinea pig, as shown here.

Feeding dish

Buy a small, ceramic bowl for your guinea pig's food. Don't use plastic ones, as they are easy to knock over and are likely to get chewed.

This kind of heavy ceramic food bowl is suitable for guinea pigs to use.

Hay

Guinea pigs love to eat fresh, dry hay, and sleep in it too. Scatter a few handfuls of soft hay over the bedding, and put a little in a hayrack attached to the hutch's door.

Using a hayrack will keep hay for eating separate from hay for sleeping.

Hutches and arks

Although they are small animals, guinea pigs need lots of space in which to sleep, run and play. The best home for a pet guinea pig is a hutch or a large cage: This page tells you about keeping guinea pigs outside in a hutch.

Size and position

A single guinea pig needs a hutch at least 90cm (3ft) wide and 45cm (1½ft) tall. The more guinea pigs you have, the bigger the hutch you will need. Put the hutch in a spot that's not too sunny or cold, and is protected from the wind. It must be raised off the ground so that cats, foxes and other animals can't open the door.

The roof should be covered in felt, and sloping at an angle to keep rain from gathering on top.

Preparing the hutch

Line the floor of the hutch with large sheets of paper, then spread bedding around 5cm (2in) deep on top. Finally, add a large clump of hay. You must change your guinea pig's bedding at least twice a week, and its hay every day.

Guinea pigs don't like smelly bedding, so remember to change it regularly.

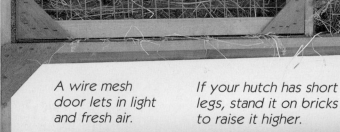

A wire mesh door lets in light and fresh air.

If your hutch has short legs, stand it on bricks to raise it higher.

The hutch needs a separate area where your guinea pig can sleep and hide away in peace.

A grazing ark

You should let your pet out every day to run around and nibble grass. A guinea pig roaming freely might get lost or hurt, so put it in a wooden grazing ark at least 1.5m (5ft) long by 90cm (3ft) wide. Never leave your guinea pig alone for a long time in an ark, as dangerous animals might try to get in while you're not looking.

Grazing arks have a covered area away from the sun and rain. Add a little hay so your guinea pig can sleep there if it wants.

Wire mesh sides let in air and stop your pet from escaping.

Put a little food and a full water bottle in the ark.

Setting up

Place the ark in an area that is sheltered from strong wind and sunlight, and where there is lots of healthy grass to eat.

Make sure you don't put the ark over any flowers, such as buttercups or poppies. Most flowers are poisonous to guinea pigs.

Return your guinea pig to its hutch at the end of the day. Move the ark to a fresh patch of grass, ready for tomorrow.

Settling in

Your guinea pig might be scared if it's leaving its mother for the first time. Two or more babies will comfort each other, but no matter how many guinea pigs you buy, they will need a little help to settle into their new home.

Getting ready

Before you bring your new pet home, have fresh bedding, hay, food and water ready in its cage. Leave your guinea pig alone for the first day so it can get used to the unfamiliar sights and smells.

Arranging its bedding makes a guinea pig feel more at home.

Help your guinea pig get used to you by offering it a tidbit in your hand.

Taming

Guinea pigs that are never handled become nervous around people. After your pet has settled in, you should try to get it used to your scent, voice and touch. The more time you spend together, the friendlier it will become.

Picking up

When your guinea pig is used to taking food from you, try picking it up. First, gently place one hand underneath the guinea pig's body, then support its bottom with your other hand. Lift it up and hold it close to you.

If your guinea pig is happy to be picked up, stroke it gently as you hold it.

For a link to a website where you can find hints and tips on how to pick up a guinea pig, go to **www.usborne-quicklinks.com**

Other pets

Dogs and cats frighten guinea pigs, so keep them apart.

This rabbit and guinea pig are friends, but these two kinds of animals must not be kept together.

If you already have a guinea pig and want to buy another, get a young one. Adult guinea pigs are more likely to welcome a new baby. Rabbits and guinea pigs can graze together, but don't keep them in the same hutch. An angry rabbit can badly injure a guinea pig

Meeting friends

When your guinea pig has become used to you and your home, try introducing it to your family and friends. Show them the right way to pick up and hold a guinea pig first.

Young children should hold a guinea pig near floor level, for safety.

Feeling safe

A relaxed guinea pig will sit in your lap or cuddle up to your chest. But if it starts to struggle or squeal, carefully put it back in its cage and leave it in peace for a while.

gurgle...

gurgle...

Happy, contented guinea pigs usually make gurgling noises as you pet them.

11

Feeding

Guinea pigs need a variety of dried and fresh food in their diet. Start off giving your pet the same kind of food it had before you bought it, then try introducing it to new kinds.

Dried food

Pet stores sell dry pellets for guinea pigs that are full of the things they need to eat, such as plants and seeds. Don't buy any other kinds of rodent foods, as they're too large and firm for guinea pigs to digest.

Keep dried food fresh by storing it in a container with a lid, like the one here.

This guinea pig food contains a mixture of healthy things, such as dried carrots, seeds and peas.

Timing

If you feed your guinea pig at the same time every day, it will soon learn when to expect dinner.

Feed your guinea pig dried food in the morning and fresh food in the afternoon. Guinea pigs don't hoard food like squirrels or hamsters do, so they need a fresh supply every day.

How much?

Your guinea pig will eat until it's full. If it leaves lots of food, give it less the next day.

When you feed your guinea pig, fill the bowl to the top. It will only eat as much food as it needs. As long as a guinea pig gets lots of exercise, it won't become too fat.

Types of teeth

The kinds of foods your guinea pig eats need to be thoroughly chewed. A guinea pig's front teeth are designed for biting food into pieces, and the strong back teeth mash it up.

There's a gap behind a guinea pig's front teeth, where food is held before it's chewed up.

Grazing

Guinea pigs love to graze on fresh grass. To make sure it gets the grass it needs, let your guinea pig out in a grazing ark every day (see page 9).

If it's not possible to let your guinea pig out, you can feed it fresh grass clippings instead. Check that they have not been sprayed with any chemicals first.

Hay

Hay is dried grass. Your guinea pig will munch on it all day, so always provide plenty. It should be soft hay, with no sharp ends.

Eating droppings

Don't worry if you see your guinea pig eating its droppings. Guinea pigs can't take all the goodness from food the first time they eat, so they make soft droppings that they can eat and digest again.

Guinea pigs make both soft and dry droppings. They only eat the soft kind.

These guinea pigs are grazing outside. Guinea pigs can safely eat a few daisies as well as fresh grass.

Fresh foods

Wild guinea pigs are herbivores, which means they eat plants, but not meat. You must feed your pet vegetables, fruit and grass, along with dried food. Never give a guinea pig sweet things such as chocolate, or it might become very sick.

Eat your greens

Your guinea pig should eat fresh, green vegetables, such as broccoli, every day. Avoid giving it lettuce or spinach, though, as they can cause upset tummies. Make sure every kind of vegetable you offer is clean and not going bad.

This is roughly the right amount of fruit and vegetables to give a pair of guinea pigs each day.

Vitamin C

Guinea pigs need to eat foods that are rich in vitamin C. Without it, they develop a skin disease called scurvy. Dried guinea pig food usually has added vitamin C, but the best source is fresh fruit.

Here are some fruits and vegetables that your guinea pig might enjoy.

Brussels sprouts

Pear

Grapes

Watermelon

Banana

Broccoli

14

Preparing fresh food

Wash the fruit and vegetables to get rid of any chemicals. Carefully cut it into slices or chunks.

Every afternoon, give your guinea pig two or three pieces of fresh food in a clean feeding bowl.

Before bedtime, throw away any uneaten food. If it starts to rot, it could make your guinea pig sick.

New food

Some guinea pigs are fussy eaters. When you give your guinea pig a type of food it hasn't tried before, only offer a small amount. If it ignores the food or doesn't eat much, it probably doesn't like it.

Guinea pigs sniff things to find out if they are good to eat. This guinea pig is deciding if it likes apples.

An indoor guinea pig

A guinea pig that lives indoors is more likely to stay healthy than a guinea pig that is kept outside. Indoor guinea pigs still need exercise and regular grazing time in an ark, though. Before you let your pet out of its cage, you must make sure there is nothing in the room that can hurt it.

A guinea pig cage

A pair of guinea pigs needs a cage at least 75 x 90cm (30 x 36in) in size. It should have a plastic bottom, lined with paper and bedding in the same way as a hutch (see page 8). Add a pile of hay or a wooden nesting box where the guinea pigs can sleep and hide away if they need to.

Where to put the cage

Guinea pigs can make a lot of noise, so don't keep the cage in your bedroom, or your pets will wake you up in the night. Put the cage in a place where the surrounding area is easy to clean, such as the corner of the room.

Guinea pigs like to kick their bedding through the bars.

Keep the cage away from:
- radiators and fires
- direct sunlight
- windows and doors
- damp places
- TVs, radios and stereos
- other pets

A guinea pig cage can have metal bars, or plastic sides like this one.

For a link to a website where you can play a fun, animated game with guinea pigs, go to **www.usborne-quicklinks.com**

Exploring

If you let your guinea pig out of its cage to exercise, check the room beforehand for possible dangers. Warn everyone in your family that your guinea pig is loose, so no one accidentally steps on it, and keep the door of the room closed. Always watch your pet closely whenever it's out of its cage.

These guinea pigs are looking around before they explore.

Spotting dangers

Don't let your guinea pig near any objects that are hot or sharp.

Guinea pigs will chew anything, so keep electric wires out of their reach.

Put houseplants where your guinea pig can't nibble them. They could be poisonous.

Toilet habits

Guinea pigs usually go to the toilet in one corner of their cage, but it's a good idea to put newspaper on the floor before letting them out. Never shout at a guinea pig for making a mess. It won't stop it from doing it again, and it might become scared of you.

If your guinea pig has an accident, wipe the spot clean with a warm, soapy cloth.

17

Play and exercise

Guinea pigs are playful and curious animals with lots of energy, so they need plenty of exercise and playtime. Pet stores sell toys for guinea pigs, although household objects, such as boxes with holes cut in them, also provide hours of fun.

A homemade obstacle course like this one, with cardboard tubes, boxes and cushions, will keep your guinea pigs amused.

Guinea pig toys

Toys can be as inexpensive and simple as a ping-pong ball, and your guinea pig will still enjoy them. But don't give your guinea pig toys designed for other animals, such as cats, as it might chew them up and choke on the small parts.

Rubbing

When your guinea pig is out of its cage, you might see it rubbing against things. This marks them with a scent that other guinea pigs can smell, but you can't. Any area with this scent is the guinea pig's territory, which means it's a place where it feels safe.

Guinea pigs rub their bottoms or chins against something to mark it as theirs.

For a link to a website where you can find
a guide to toys that guinea pigs enjoy,
go to **www.usborne-quicklinks.com**

Jumping for joy

You may sometimes see your guinea pig leap straight
up into the air while arching its back, or run across
the floor and make several shorter jumps one after
the other. This is called popcorn jumping, and it's
the sign of a healthy and happy guinea pig.

*Happy guinea
pigs are real
acrobats,
performing
excited hops
and leaps.*

Running around

Guinea pigs need regular
exercise to keep them from
becoming overweight and
unhealthy. Let your guinea pig
out of its hutch or cage at least
three times a week and put
it in a run, a grazing ark
or any enclosed place
where it can't escape.

*Running around in the
fresh air will help these
guinea pigs to stay fit.*

Catching your pet

When your guinea pig has finished playing or exercising,
you'll need to return it to its home for a rest.

*Guinea pigs are easily
tempted by fresh fruit.*

Leave the hutch door open
with a ramp down to the
ground. Your guinea pig
might come back in by itself.

If your pet doesn't want
to return to its hutch, or
you can't wait, try coaxing
it in with a tasty snack.

Don't shout at your guinea
pig, or chase after it. A
frightened guinea pig is
less likely to come to you.

Housekeeping

A guinea pig in a dirty, smelly environment is more likely to become sick. You should clean out your pet's cage or hutch two or three times a week, and keep its bedding fresh.

This guinea pig is having fun tearing up its new bedding.

Dirty bedding

Most guinea pigs use one corner of their living area as a toilet. If the bedding becomes soggy or smelly in this area, throw it away and replace it with a fresh handful each day.

Wrap smelly old bedding in newspaper before you throw it away.

Cage cleaning

Empty the used bedding and any old food out of your guinea pig's cage, and wash the plastic tray with mild dishwashing liquid. Rinse it thoroughly, making sure there are no dirty bits left behind, then dry it with an old towel. Put in clean bedding and hay. Wash the food bowl and water bottle, too.

If you have a cage with a plastic top instead of metal bars, wash that part as well as the tray.

For a link to a website where you can take a quiz
to find out how much you know about guinea
pigs, go to **www.usborne-quicklinks.com**

Hutch cleaning

Use disinfectant that's safe for guinea pigs. You can buy this in pet stores.

1. Throw away the hay, old bedding and paper. Use a spatula or dustpan and brush to remove the dirt.

2. Dip a brush into some warm, soapy water. Scrub the inside of the hutch and rinse it with clean water.

3. Let the hutch dry. Spray it with disinfectant. Lay paper in the bottom, then cover it with fresh bedding and hay.

It's a good idea to clean your guinea pig's home while it's out grazing.

4. Use a bottle brush to scrub the water bottle with soapy water. Rinse it well.

Always remember to wash your hands thoroughly when you've finished cleaning.

What does it mean?

Guinea pigs use sounds and body language to let each other know how they feel. If you watch your pet and listen carefully to it, you will soon be able to understand what it's trying to say.

Sniffing

A guinea pig learns a lot from its keen sense of smell. When guinea pigs meet for the first time, they sniff each other to decide if they are friends.

This guinea pig is sniffing the air to find out what's going on around it.

Making noises

Guinea pigs use a wide range of noises to express themselves.

A happy guinea pig purrs, or makes a soft chortling noise.

An unhappy guinea pig will make a loud, high-pitched squeak.

A rumbling sound means your guinea pig is annoyed. If you are handling it when it does this, put it down.

When guinea pigs are excited, they give out a loud "wheeek!"

Male guinea pigs "rumblestrut" when they want to show off. They sway their hips while making a low purr.

For links to websites where you can listen to lots of guinea pig noises, go to **www.usborne-quicklinks.com**

Staying still

A very frightened guinea pig will stand still, like a statue. If you see your guinea pig frozen like this, leave it alone until it starts to move again, or you might scare it more.

When a wild guinea pig sees a dangerous animal, it freezes like this. Standing still makes it harder to spot.

Fighting

Guinea pigs sometimes get angry with each other. If they are preparing to fight, they will start by fluffing out their hair and making an angry chattering sound. They then bare their teeth in a wide yawn.

You can stop guinea pigs from attacking each other by throwing a towel over them. They become confused, and lose the urge to fight.

If a pair of guinea pigs has had a fight, they must be kept in separate cages afterwards. They will not make friends again.

Mysterious chirps

Very occasionally, a guinea pig will stand still and make a noise like a chirping bird, sometimes for several minutes. No one but the guinea pig knows what this strange action means.

chirp chirp chirp

All other guinea pigs nearby will stop and listen if a companion starts to chirp.

23

Baby guinea pigs

When they are a few months old, guinea pigs are ready to have babies. Never try to breed guinea pigs without expert advice. The babies may look sweet, but you'll have to find new homes for them, and make sure no more babies are born.

Newborn babies

Baby guinea pigs are called puppies. A mother guinea pig can have up to five puppies at a time.

Unlike most rodents, baby guinea pigs are born with fur and open eyes, and can walk within an hour or two. They are about as big as an adult mouse.

This mother guinea pig will lick her newborn babies clean.

Mealtime

At first, the puppies drink milk from their mother. She only has two nipples, so they must take turns. After a few days, the puppies start to eat dry foods.

The smallest puppy might struggle to get enough milk from its mother.

Helpful aunties

In the wild, a mother guinea pig is surrounded by her sisters and cousins, who will help to raise her young. These other females protect the puppies.

Guinea pig puppies are cared for by many members of their family.

Happy families

At two weeks old, the puppies are very loving. They play together, huddle up for warmth, and make noises to let each other know where they are.

A puppy who becomes separated from its family will get anxious and look for them.

The puppies make a "hut hut hut" noise to let their sisters and brothers know where they are.

Leaving home

Male guinea pigs should be kept in separate cages from their mother and sisters when they reach five weeks old. If not, they will fight or try to make more babies. Female puppies can stay with their mother.

One male puppy can go and live in a separate cage with his father when he's a few weeks old.

Mini adults

Guinea pig puppies are fully grown at one year old, but they look like adults much sooner than this.

The third guinea pig from the left is the mother of the others, but her month-old puppies look almost as old as she does.

25

Grooming

Guinea pigs are naturally clean animals, and groom themselves regularly. They lick their fur, and run their teeth and claws through it like a comb. You can help keep your pet in tip-top condition by brushing, combing and washing it too.

This guinea pig is licking its back to clean its fur.

Before you groom and wash your guinea pig, make sure you have all of these things:

- soft brush
- wide-toothed comb
- large plastic bowl
- jug of warm (NOT hot) water
- shampoo for guinea pigs (you can buy this from a pet store)
- towel
- hot-water bottle
- carrying box

Brushing and combing

Use one hand to keep your guinea pig still.

Put down a towel for your guinea pig to sit on. Get it in a comfortable position in your lap, or on a low surface.

Brush the hair in the direction it grows.

Brush the hair on its back away from its head. Gently brush its tummy, and under its chin. Don't tug.

Your guinea pig will enjoy being groomed, as long as you're gentle.

After brushing, comb the hair on its back, then under its chin. Carefully untangle any knots.

For a link to a website where you can watch
guinea pigs on videos and live webcams,
go to **www.usborne-quicklinks.com**

Bathing

Help keep your pet clean and healthy by
giving it a bath every three months or so.

*Talk quietly to
your guinea
pig to calm
it down.*

Lower your guinea pig into
a large, plastic bowl half-
filled with warm water.
Hold it firmly, but gently.

*Don't get any shampoo in
your guinea pig's eyes
and nose.*

Splash water on its coat.
Pour a capful of shampoo
onto its back, and gently
rub it into the hair all over.

*Hold up your guinea
pig's head as you
pour the water.*

Pour warm water over your
guinea pig's neck, and rub
it in. Keep pouring until all
the shampoo has gone.

Drying off

After washing your guinea pig, lift it
onto the towel. Fold the towel over
your pet and rub its coat gently,
giving it a thorough brush
afterwards. Put your guinea
pig inside its carrying box
with a hot-water bottle
wrapped in a dry towel,
and keep the box in
a warm room until
your pet is dry.

*This guinea pig
is drying off
after a bath.*

Keeping healthy

Your guinea pig can't tell you when it's feeling unwell, so you must watch it carefully for signs that something is wrong. Most problems can be treated at home, but some will need a trip to the vet (see page 30).

Sore skin

Guinea pigs often suffer from skin infections, which make them very uncomfortable. If bald, scaly or sore patches start to appear on your pet's body, treat it with skin oil or shampoo. You can buy these from a vet or a pet store.

A guinea pig that bites or scratches itself like this might have a skin problem.

Mites and lice

Guinea pigs rarely catch fleas. A guinea pig that's scratching a lot is more likely to have mites or lice. Like fleas, these are little creatures that live in an animal's fur and make it itch.

Wear old gloves to put your guinea pig in its carrying box, and thoroughly clean its cage. Wash its fur with anti-pest shampoo. If you have more than one guinea pig, you'll need to wash them all.

You can get rid of mites and lice using medicated shampoo for small animals.

Lice are too small to see clearly. This drawing shows one bigger so you can see what its shape is like.

General health

Your guinea pig might be unwell if its breathing is wheezy, or if it doesn't want to eat or drink.

A guinea pig with a cold might develop a more serious illness, unless it receives treatment.

A shivering guinea pig with a runny nose and eyes might have a cold. It should be seen by a vet at once.

If your guinea pig is wounded, wash the wound with warm water and apply a little antiseptic ointment.

Heatstroke

Guinea pigs need a shady place to hide in hot weather, or else they get sick. A guinea pig that is gasping and lying flat on its tummy might have heatstroke. Wrap your pet in a towel soaked with cold water until it cools down. Don't give it anything to drink until its breathing returns to normal, or it could choke.

A sick guinea pig will need to rest. Give it some extra hay to make a warm, safe bed like this one.

As soon as your guinea pig stops gasping and starts to recover, take the damp towel away.

Visiting the vet

As long as you take good care of your guinea pig and feed it the right things, it should stay healthy. But if it looks very poorly, or needs its teeth and claws clipped, you should take your guinea pig to a vet.

Serious problems

You must contact a vet as quickly as possible if your guinea pig's droppings are runny, or it can't breathe properly. These are both signs that something might be seriously wrong.

Claws and teeth

If your guinea pig is having difficulty running around, a vet may need to clip its claws. Teeth can also be clipped by a vet, if they have become too long. Overgrown teeth make it hard for a guinea pig to eat.

Here, a vet is using clippers to trim a guinea pig's claws. This doesn't hurt the guinea pig.

Making the journey

Take your guinea pig to the vet in its carrying box, with a little hay in the bottom. Put an old blanket on the car seat to avoid mess. Keep your guinea pig in its box while you wait to see the vet, so it won't be scared by the other animals at the clinic.

Talk to your guinea pig to calm it down as you prepare for the journey.

A guinea pig's teeth will probably not need clipping if it has enough hard things to gnaw.

Keep the carrying box as still as you can while the car is moving, to stop your pet from being jolted around.

Going away

For a link to a website where you can send electronic guinea pig greeting cards, go to **www.usborne-quicklinks.com**

You can leave a guinea pig by itself for one night, as long as it has food and water. If you are going away for longer, ask a friend to look after your pet until you return. Try to ask someone who already knows about guinea pigs.

This guinea pig is still getting the fresh foods it needs while its owner is away.

Before you go

You'll need to tell your friend what times to give your guinea pig food, and how much it needs. Explain how to clean out the cage, too, and how to recognize if the guinea pig is unwell.

Write your friend a list of the things your pet needs.

Getting to a friend

You will need to take your guinea pig to your friend's house if they can't visit your home every day. Take food, bedding and cleaning equipment, along with the hutch or cage. Remember to wash them first.

Other guinea pigs

If your friend has guinea pigs already, yours might fight with them if they are put together. Guinea pigs of opposite sexes might even try to have babies. Ask your friend to make sure they are kept apart.

Transport your guinea pig in its carrying box. Give your friend everything that's needed to look after your pet.

Your guinea pig will feel less nervous if you leave it something with a familiar smell, such as a handful of old hay.

Index

Cover design by Michael Hill

With thanks to Donna Bennett

Copyright © 2005 Usborne Publishing Ltd.
First published in 2005 by Usborne Publishing Ltd, 83–85 Saffron Hill, London EC1N 8RT, England. www.usborne.com
All rights reserved. No part of this publication may be reproduced, stored in a retrieval system, or transmitted in any form or by any means, electronic, mechanical, photocopying, recording or otherwise, without the prior permission of the publisher.
The name Usborne and the devices ♀ 🐝 are Trade Marks of Usborne Publishing Ltd.
Printed in China. UE. First published in America in 2005.